A Pet's Life

Rabbits

Anita Ganeri

Heinemann Library
Chicago, Illinois

www.heinemannraintree.com
Visit our website to find out more information about Heinemann-Raintree books.

To order:
☎ Phone 888-454-2279
⌨ Visit www.heinemannraintree.com to browse our catalog and order online.

© 2009 Heinemann Library
an imprint of Capstone Global Library, LLC
Chicago, Illinois

Customer Service: 888-454-2279

Visit our website at www.heinemannraintree.com

Printed and bound by South China Printing Company Ltd

13 12 11 10 09
10 9 8 7 6 5 4 3 2

Library of Congress Cataloging-in-Publication Data
New edition ISBN: 978 14329 3394 4 (hardcover) – 978 14329 3401 9 (paperback)
The Library of Congress has cataloged the first edition as follows:
Ganeri, Anita, 1961-
   Rabbits / Anita Ganeri.
      v. cm. -- (A pet's life) (Heinemann first library)
Includes bibliographical references and index.
Contents: What is a rabbit? -- Rabbit babies -- Your pet rabbit --
Choosing your rabbit -- Setting up your cage -- Rabbit play-time --
Welcome home -- Feeding time -- Cleaning the cage -- Growing up -- A
healthy rabbit -- Old age.
   ISBN 1-4034-3995-8 (Hardcover) -- ISBN 1-4034-4274-6 (pbk.)
   1. Rabbits--Juvenile literature. [1. Rabbits as pets. 2. Pets.] I. Title. II. Series.
   SF453.2.G36 2003
   636.9'322--dc21
                                2002151593

Acknowledgments
The author and publishers are grateful to the following for permission to reproduce copyright material:
Ardea pp. **5**, **6**, **7** (John Daniels); © Capstone Global Library Ltd pp. **11**, **12**, **13**, **14**, **15**, **16**, **17**, **18**, **19**, **22**, **23**, **24**, **25**, **26**, **27** (Tudor Photography); Chris Honeywell p. **10**; RSPCA p. **4** (E A Janes); Warren Photographic pp. **8**, **9**, **20**, **21** (Jane Burton).

Cover photograph of a lop-eared rabbit reproduced with permission of Naturepl.com. (© Aflo).

The publishers would like to thank Judy Tuma for her invaluable assistance in the preparation of this book.

Every effort has been made to contact copyright holders of any material reproduced in this book. Any omissions will be rectified in subsequent printings if notice is given to the publisher.

Contents

Some words are shown in bold, **like this**. You can find out what they mean by looking in the Glossary.

What Do Rabbits Look Like?

Rabbits can have long or short fur. Their fur can be black, white, grey, or golden brown. Some rabbits have long, straight ears, and some have long, floppy ears.

Rabbits come in many different sizes. These small rabbits are named Netherland Dwarfs.

This picture shows the different parts of a rabbit's body. You can see what each part is used for.

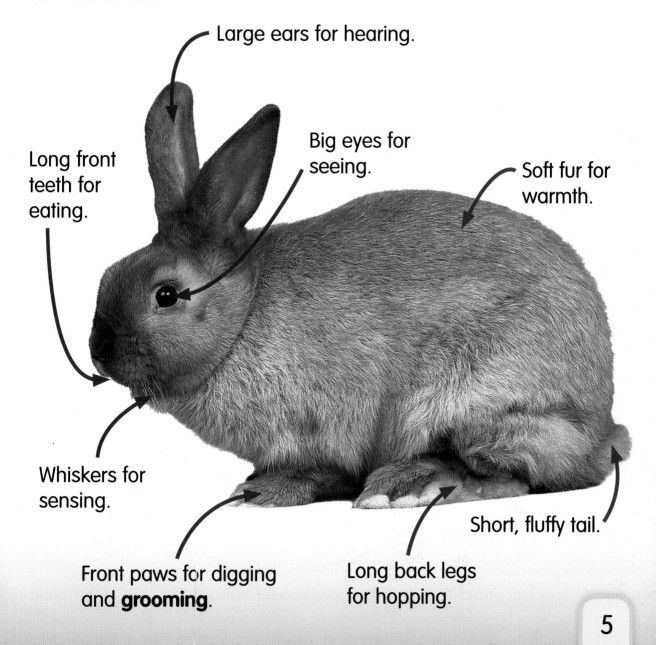

Large ears for hearing.

Big eyes for seeing.

Soft fur for warmth.

Long front teeth for eating.

Whiskers for sensing.

Front paws for digging and **grooming**.

Long back legs for hopping.

Short, fluffy tail.

Rabbit Babies

Baby rabbits are called kits. They are born with no fur and with their eyes closed. A mother rabbit may have as many as eight babies in a **litter**. Don't disturb rabbit kits.

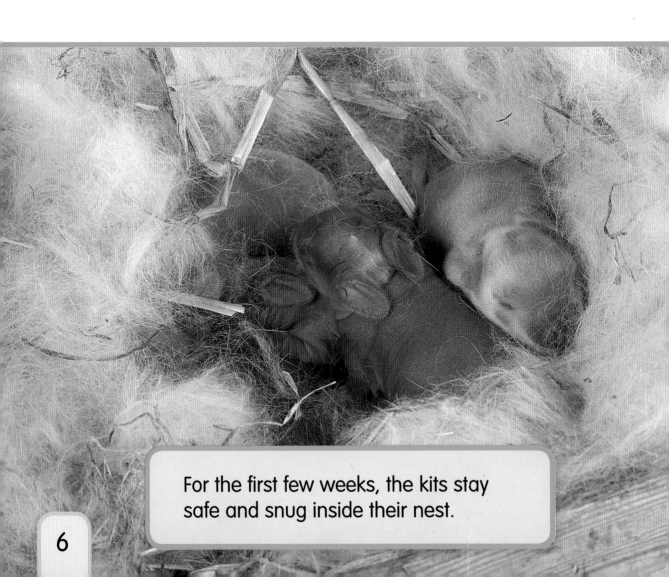

For the first few weeks, the kits stay safe and snug inside their nest.

Rabbits can have lots of babies. It is best to keep male and female rabbits apart.

The kits are old enough to leave their mother when they are about five weeks old. Then they are ready to become pets.

Choosing Your Rabbits

Animal shelters are often looking for good homes for rabbits. You can also buy rabbits from pet stores or from rabbit **breeders**.

Rabbits get lonely, so keep two together. It is best to keep two **neutered** female rabbits.

Choose rabbits that look healthy and lively. They should have glossy coats, clear, bright eyes, and clean teeth and ears.

A rabbit with a runny nose may be sick. This rabbit looks healthy.

Your Rabbits' Cage

Your rabbits need a roomy cage to live in. The rabbit cage should have two rooms – one to live in and one for sleeping.

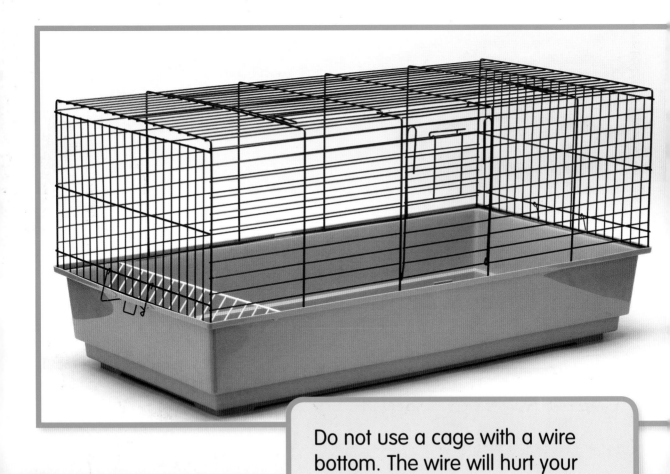

Do not use a cage with a wire bottom. The wire will hurt your rabbits' paws.

Rabbits stay healthier if they are kept indoors.

Line the bottom of the cage with newspaper. Cover it with unscented wood **shavings**. A good pile of shredded paper or straw makes a cozy bed.

Welcome Home

You can take your rabbits home in a strong carrying box. Your rabbits will need some time alone to settle into their new home.

Be sure that the carrying box has air holes in it so that your rabbits can breathe.

Always pick up a rabbit properly. Put one hand under the rabbit's body, under its shoulders. Put your other hand under its bottom. Then lift it up close to you.

Hold your rabbit close to your body to support its weight.

Playing With Your Rabbits

Rabbits need plenty of exercise. Play with them in a room that is safe for them. Do not put house plants where your rabbits can reach them.

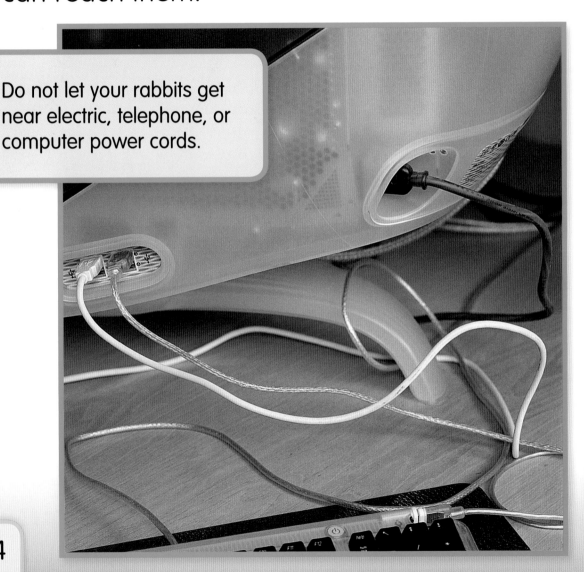

Do not let your rabbits get near electric, telephone, or computer power cords.

Play with your rabbits every day.
Otherwise they will get bored.

When they are out of their cage, keep your
rabbits in the safe room. Do not let other
animals in the room with your rabbits.

Feeding Time

Pet stores sell special food pellets for rabbits. Rabbits also like to nibble on raw fruits and vegetables, such as apples, carrots, and cabbage.

Rabbits also like broccoli, turnips, parsley, and dandelion leaves.

Feed your rabbits two small meals a day, in the morning and in the evening. Put the food in heavy bowls so that your rabbits cannot tip them over.

Rabbits should have fresh water and hay available at all times.

Cleaning the Cage

Rabbits are clean animals and do not like to live in a dirty cage. Remove wet bedding and **droppings** every day. Wash their water bottle and food bowls every day, too.

Once a week, sweep the cage out.

Always wash your hands after cleaning out your rabbits' cage.

Once a week, wash the cage with warm, soapy water, and rinse it with clean water. Make sure the cage is dry before you put your rabbits back inside.

Growing Up

Some rabbits grow very large. When you choose your rabbits, find out how big they will grow. Large rabbits need more space than small or medium-size rabbits.

You may need to get a bigger rabbit cage as your rabbits grow up.

Rabbits noses twitch when they smell other rabbits to find out if they are friends.

The sounds and movements your rabbits make are their ways of talking. Rabbits stamp their back feet if they are angry or frightened.

Healthy Rabbits

You should check with a **veterinarian** if your rabbits look sick. A runny nose, runny eyes, a dirty bottom, or not eating may be signs of sickness.

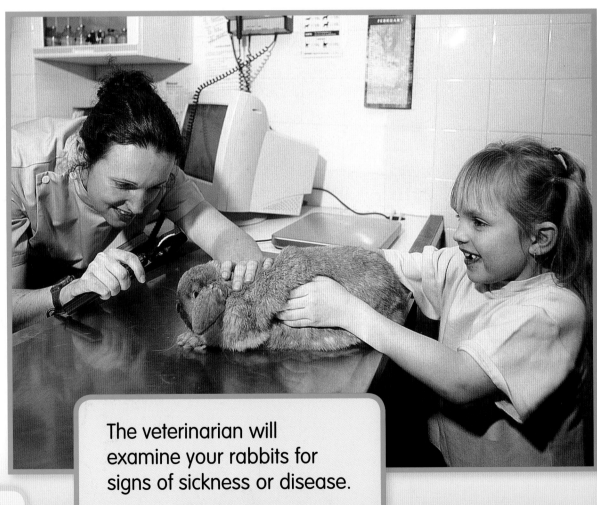

The veterinarian will examine your rabbits for signs of sickness or disease.

Only a veterinarian or an adult should give medicines to your rabbits.

If your rabbits start scratching or biting their fur a lot, they might have mites or fleas. The veterinarian will tell you how to take care of these problems.

Your Pet Rabbits

Rabbits are fun to keep as pets but they need lots of care and exercise. You must be a good pet owner and learn to look after your rabbits properly.

Rabbits are very friendly and love to be stroked.

Show your friend exactly how you care for your pets.

When you go on vacation, ask a friend or neighbor to take care of your rabbits. Write a list of what they should do. Be sure to include the number of your pets' **veterinarian**.

Old Age

If you look after your rabbits, they may live for up to ten or twelve years. Take your rabbits to the **veterinarian** every six months for a checkup to make sure they stay healthy.

Older rabbits still need exercise to help them stay healthy and not gain too much weight.

Older rabbits may be less active than young rabbits. Your older rabbits will still like to be played with and stroked.

Caring for your rabbits will help you learn how to treat animals properly.

Useful Tips

- A rabbit's front teeth grow all the time. Give your pets a wooden block to **gnaw** on to stop their teeth from growing too long.

- Your rabbits may need their nails clipped from time to time. The **veterinarian** will do this for you.

- Rabbits **groom** themselves to keep their fur clean. But you need to brush long-haired rabbits every day. You can brush short-haired rabbits once a week.

- Do not keep other types of animals in the same cage as your rabbits.

- All female rabbits need to be **spayed** and male rabbits need to be **neutered** to stop them from having babies.

Fact File

- Wild rabbits are smaller than many pet rabbits. Their fur is usually brown or gray. They dig their homes, called **burrows**, underground.

- Rabbits were first kept as pets about 400 years ago.

- There are about 100 different **breeds** of rabbits. The largest kind of pet rabbit is the Flemish giant. It is about the size of a small dog.

- Dwarf rabbits are the smallest breeds. They can weigh less than a bag of sugar.

- The largest lop-eared rabbits may have ears that are 8 inches long.

Glossary

animal shelter place where lost or unwanted animals are looked after

breed type or kind of an animal

breeder someone who raises animals

burrow hole or tunnel in the ground

disease sickness

droppings waste from the body

gnaw chew and bite

groom gently brush your rabbits' fur. Rabbits also groom themselves.

litter baby rabbits born at the same time

neutered when a male animal has an operation so that it cannot have any babies

shavings very thin slices of wood

spayed when a female animal has an operation so that it cannot have any babies

veterinarian specially trained animal doctor

More Books to Read

An older reader can help you with these books.

Boyer Binns, Tristan. *Keeping Pets: Rabbits.* Chicago, IL: Heinemann Library, 2006.

Doudna, Kelly. *Perfect Pets: Rascally Rabbits.* S. Pasadena, CA: SandCastle Publishing, 2007.

Maass, Sarah. *Caring for Your Rabbit (First Facts).* Mankato, MN: Capstone Press, 2006.

Miller, Heather. *This is What I Want To Be: Veterinarian.* Chicago, IL: Heinemann Library, 2004.

Small Pet Care: How to Look After Your Rabbit, Guinea Pig, or Hamster. New York: Dorling Kindersley Publishing Inc., 2005.

Index